For Lotta, Emely,
Jakob, Philipp, Lucas and Emil

Copyright © 2014 by kapila kommunikation

Published in the United States of America by
International Enneagram Association Publications,
an imprint of the International Enneagram Association.
Registered Offices: 4010 Executive Park Drive, Suite 100
Cincinnati, Ohio 45241 USA

ISBN 978-0-9903273-1-8

www.internationalenneagram.org

First English Edition

Idea/Text: Claudia N. Schöffler
Enneagram Counseling (German)/Text: Alfons Mayer
Illustrations: Petra Götz
Graphic Art: www.agentur-zitzmann.de
Translation: Brigitte Hansen
Enneagram Counseling (English)/Translation: CJ Fitzsimons

Claudia Schöffler · Petra Götz · Alfons Mayer

About the Wind, the Meadows and the Nine Worlds

International
ENNEAGRAM
Association

Early one morning, the Wind awoke high up in the mountains. He had blown to this range from the far South to bring the warmth of summer to the plants and animals. Right now, the Wind is very eager to meet up with his friends. Over time, they have all become very dear to him!

Each of them is very special!

Strong and powerful, the fearless Bull protects his cows and calves.

The Butterfly is always merry and ready to have fun.

The little Mouse is often fearful – after all, the world is full of dangers!

The beautiful Wild Horse loves to daydream and always looks a bit sad as she does so.

The Fox likes to keep his distance. This allows him to observe more carefully and get a clear picture in his head.

The laid-back Bear enjoys being left alone.

The Bee always feels like he has to sort everything out. What a lot of work!

The Dog loves it when the shepherd asks him to guard his sheep.

The Eagle is the King of the Skies and loves to be admired.

"Oh, there they are!" exclaims the South Wind joyfully. He gently settles in close to them and eavesdrops on their conversation.

"My work is endless!" sighs the busy Bee to herself. "I'm soooo bored," moans the Wild Horse. "I don't know what's going on today!" thinks the Fox as he hides behind a newspaper.

However the Wind can hear even more than their voices are saying. From deep within their hearts, he can hear sounds ringing out to him: "It would be so nice to have a true friend!"

"I have an idea!" the Eagle exclaims excitedly. "WE'LL HAVE A BIG PARTY! We'll invite all the animals from these mountains and each one of us will perform. Just like in the circus! What do you think?!?"
The group is seized by a momentary jolt. With inquisitive eyes, they all look at the Eagle. WHAT DO YOU MEAN? A PERFORMANCE?

"What a wonderful idea! That will bring joy to everyone's heart." Lovingly, the Wind strokes each one's head and ...

... knows what they're thinking:

The Fox knows full well what he's capable of, but doesn't want to be the focus of attention.
The Mouse is full of self-doubt, she starts to quiver but hopes that no one will notice.
The merry Butterfly is full of enthusiasm and ideas, she will choose the one that's most fun.

... sees what they're doing:

The Bull, bursting with energy, pounds his hooves
and places himself so no one can get by.
The Bee spreads her wings and gets ready – for her,
duty comes first.
The Bear rolls up into a ball and would prefer to sleep –
this is all too mouch for him.

... senses what they're feeling:

The radiant Eagle, King of the Skies, casts
his glance over the group – he is the best.
The friendly Dog rests his head between his paws,
takes a deep breath and feels happy and at ease.
The beautiful Wild Horse is lonely – she would
love to be far away in a nicer place.

"HOW is that supposed to work?!" the Bee asks herself, and feels the strain.

Frantically, she tries to come up with a solution.

"I've got it!" Eagerly, she flies back to the bee hive to discuss her idea with the others.

"Would you participate in a bee ballet? We could dance to the music of the grasshoppers." The others like this idea.

"We'll get to work immediately!" the Bee decides.

She's strict. When things don't go as planned during the numerous rehearsals, she gets really angry. Finally, she's more or less satisfied.

Only when everything has been planned and organized can the Bee look forward to the party.

perfectly

"Whether there's a public performance or
not, I just don't want to be in the spot-
light. I prefer to stay in the background
and to help the others." This scenario
makes his heart leap for joy.

"Without me, my friends wouldn't do
nearly as well!" he thinks to himself. The
Dog is so moved by this thought that it
warms his heart.

Because he's eager to *help*
everyone, the Dog is looking
forward to the party.

For Lotta, Emely,
Jakob, Philipp, Lucas and Emil

Copyright © 2014 by kapila kommunikation

All rights reserved

Published in the United States of America by
International Enneagram Association Publications,
an imprint of the International Enneagram Association.
Registered Offices: 4010 Executive Park Drive, Suite 100
Cincinnati, Ohio 45241 USA

ISBN 978-0-9903273-1-8

www.internationalenneagram.org

First English Edition

Idea/Text: Claudia N. Schöffler
Enneagram Counseling (German)/Text: Alfons Mayer
Illustrations: Petra Götz
Graphic Art: www.agentur-zitzmann.de
Translation: Brigitte Hansen
Enneagram Counseling (English)/Translation: CJ Fitzsimons

"Great, everyone will participate!" the Eagle proclaims with a touch of self-satisfaction!

Naturally, he organizes everything himself: He flies from valley to valley to invite all the animals. He discusses the crickets' musical accompaniment with the leader of their orchestra. Incidentally, he also keeps an eye out for the biggest meadow he can find for staging the event.

Now what will HE perform?

He doesn't have to think long about that. "I will swoop down from dizzying heights and take the audience's breath away. And I won't have to practice either – I already know how!"

The Eagle doesn't doubt the

success of his idea for even a second!

"I won't take part in that – especially not without a personal invitation," snorts the Wild Horse.

But then, from deep within her memory, she recalls an image of herself with a wind-blown mane as she jumped really high and far. That was an indescribably wonderful feeling!

The Wild Horse begins to daydream about performing elegant jumps in a beautiful costume of flowers. "Well, I think I will take part after all," she decides.

"I'm going to be extraordinarily beautiful!" She gallops off in high spirits to begin making the necessary arrangements.

On the evening of the party,
the Horse will be something very
special.

The Fox withdraws into the forest for three days and three nights. Then he makes a decision.

"I will perform magic! I will perform the fire trick using a glass shard. I learned it by watching the woodsmen. But I will not reveal the secret to anyone – EVER!" Off he goes to look for a glass shard.

Knowing that he will be able to demonstrate something very mysterious is incredibly satisfying for the Fox.

"Oh goodness, that all sounds so dangerous for me!"
the Mouse whispers with a quaking voice.

"Of course, I don't want to be a spoilsport either."

In this hour of need, she turns to her family. "How
about the Mouse March that we performed at
Grandpa's birthday?" suggests her older brother.

"But that was for Grandpa! I don't think I can do it
unless you practice a lot with me."

Yet even though she rehearses the routine many
times, her misgivings remain as to whether every-
thing will go smoothly.

Despite countless rehearsals the
Mouse can't relax. For her, the
whole affair will always remain
dangerous.

"Hopefully very many animals will show up so we can hold a really big party. I want everyone to be joyous and happy," the Butterfly cheers.

She makes a plan and assembles her numerous family members on the meadow of flowers. Already this get-together is turning out to be an exuberant and motley party.

"We'll amaze the audience and also make them laugh!"

Here one moment and gone the next. Her numerous sisters, brothers, cousins, aunts and uncles are given instructions to hide discretely

among the audience. Prompted by a secret signal, one of them will show themselves to the audience just before disappearing again a moment later. And straight away, another butterfly will appear at another – completely different – location. And so on and so forth ...

Things should always be this *fun*
– not only on this evening.

"Why does everyone listen to what the Eagle says," the Bull fumes. "I'm the STRONGEST, I'm the BOSS."

He nervously flexes his muscles. He'll show them all! "I'll lift a giant boulder off the ground with my horns and hurl it through the air."

The Bull trains hard. While some of those watching him are frightened, others are very impressed.

Suddenly the Mouse shouts out: "WATCH OUT!"

At the very moment that the Eagle prepares to land, a boulder flies through the air – right into the Eagle's path of flight.

"You could have killed me!" the Eagle shouts. "Well, if YOU'RE stupid enough to fly about here. This is where I train!" The Bull takes a step toward the Eagle.

The Eagle quickly comes to his senses, "If I fight with the Bull now, I will endanger the party. I certainly don't want to do that." Cleverly, he backs down.

The Bull loves to be

in charge,

the party itself isn't that important to him.

"What's all the fuss about?" growls the bear. Even the thought of having to do something for the party is strenuous for him. He'd rather just doze!

"I have an idea – let's juggle! We'll make our own balls, juggling clubs and colorful bands.", Mrs. Bear's loud voice penetrates his ears. How annoying!

Since the Bear always lets himself get distracted by other things, everything takes forever.

The Bear is looking forward to the evening, he feels at ease and everything is so *harmonious.*

Finally the big evening has arrived! Guests pour in from everywhere. The Wind has found an especially good perch in a treetop.

There, the crickets have begun to play their opening concert ...

*The audience cheers the
Butterfly's performance!
How can she appear in
different places at virtually
the same time?*

*The Bull's
performance
is eagerly awaited.
The boulder flies
through the air.
After a few
seconds of silence,
thunderous applause
fills the air.*

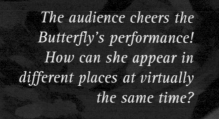

*The Eagle is exhilarated by his downward swoops! He doesn't
even notice how some members of the audience shake their
heads in disbelief in the face of such daring.*

*As she marches,
the Mouse over-
comes her fear
and becomes quite
courageous. Yet she
is still very relieved
and happy when her
performance is over.*

*The Bear executes
true artistic feats
with whimsical
colorful balls, bands
und juggling clubs.
"I'm surprised at
how adept he can
be," remarks the
delighted Mrs. Bear.*

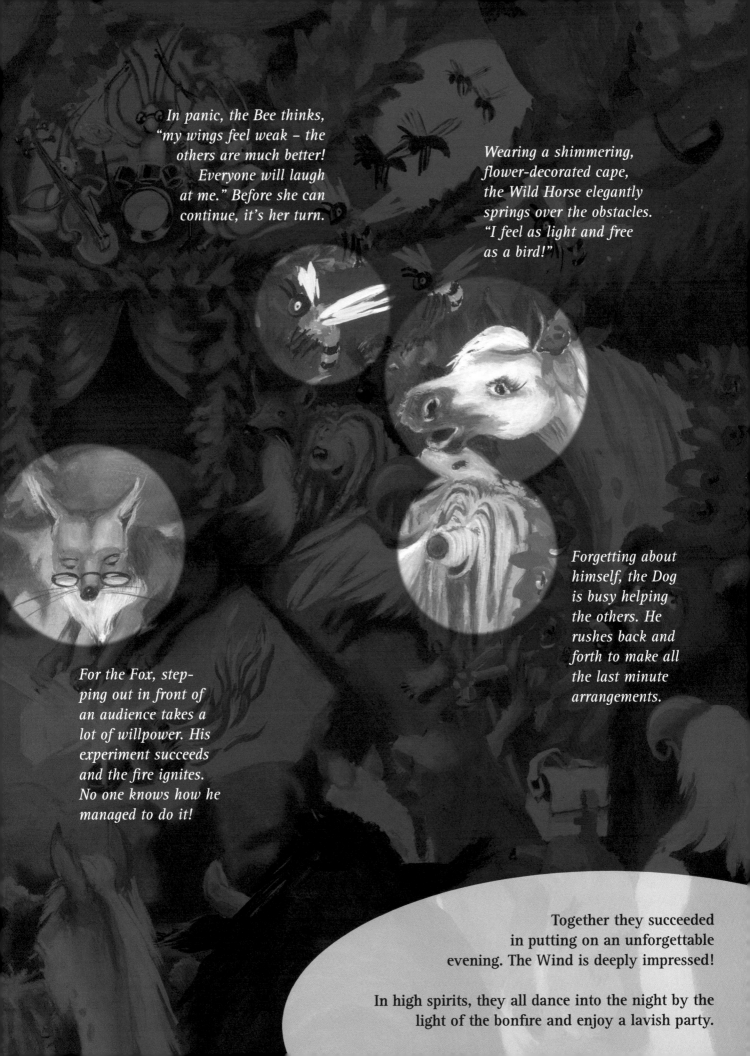

In panic, the Bee thinks, "my wings feel weak – the others are much better! Everyone will laugh at me." Before she can continue, it's her turn.

Wearing a shimmering, flower-decorated cape, the Wild Horse elegantly springs over the obstacles. "I feel as light and free as a bird!"

Forgetting about himself, the Dog is busy helping the others. He rushes back and forth to make all the last minute arrangements.

For the Fox, stepping out in front of an audience takes a lot of willpower. His experiment succeeds and the fire ignites. No one knows how he managed to do it!

Together they succeeded in putting on an unforgettable evening. The Wind is deeply impressed!

In high spirits, they all dance into the night by the light of the bonfire and enjoy a lavish party.

The next morning, they are all together and enjoying the peaceful atmosphere. They are still dwelling on the events that unfolded the previous evening ...

"Something is different! But what?" wonders the Wind. "Where did the Eagle leave his chain? What's the Butterfly doing with a newspaper? After all, it belongs to the Fox!"

Astonishingly, the Fox is not on his own but is sitting close to the others. He's impressed with the Bull's drive and directness. He thinks wistfully, "If I could only observe less and participate more – and also say what I think sometimes."

"A lot is good, but even more is better! That's not always quite true," reflects the Butterfly. "The Fox gets by with so little. Occasionally, I'd like to be able to do that." She decides that she would like to do something with him. Just the two of them!

The Bee can't help giggling while thin[king] about the Butterfly['s] performance. "Ho[w] wonderful to be ab[le] to make other peo[ple] laugh!" Then she flies off to see her.

The Dog is happy not to have to take care of the others anymore. He senses just how soothing that can be. He steals a glance at the beautiful Horse who feels no need to follow the others.

From deep within, the Bull belches, "Actually, it's kind of nice not to have to be in charge all the time." It's hard for him to believe that Dog declined to give his own performance. "Tomorrow, I'll help him protect the sheep."

"It was great, just great," thinks the Mouse with a sense of relief. "Throughout all the excitement, the Bear managed to stay calm and peaceful." As she snuggles up close to him, it strikes her that he seems to have no fear.

"Without the Eagle, we wouldn't have had such a splendid evening!" The Bear decides that, in the near future, he will turn his great ideas into deeds.

The Eagle is very proud that the evening turned out to be such a success – it was, after all, his idea! He turns his gaze to the Mouse. In spite of all her doubts, she didn't let the others down because they are all very important to her. "Would I have done the same?" he asks himself.

Still completely enraptured by the events of the previous evening, the Wild Horse catches sight of the Bee and ponders, "I wonder if she could teach me how to see things clearly and to complete tasks more promptly."

"Well, now I can see what's different", marvels the Wind. "Each animal also harbors something from one of the other animals within them: a keepsake!" They each opened their hearts and were able to make a precious discovery through one of the others. That's friendship! Wonderful!

Afterword for the big people

These nine animals mirror the nine different personality types of the Enneagram (Greek: ennea=9, gram=image, letter). They represent the nine facets of the soul and define the very essence of a person's being. Each of the nine images exemplifies its own world, in other words, a "typical" way of feeling, thinking and acting that is sustained by a central objective that we pursue throughout our lives. People are different and tick in different ways and, from the perspective of the Enneagram, this is completely normal. Thus, of the many people that we encounter during the course of our lives, there are those with whom we share traits and those who are essentially different from us.

Young or old, boy or girl, man or woman, each of us lives in our own world. We are closer to and more familiar with some worlds, while other worlds puzzle us –
we experience them as extraordinarily alien.
Another person can be so different to me!

At that moment when we parents, day-care providers or teachers recognize our children in their particular world, we can finally see who they really are – and they feel understood.
This also applies, in the same way, to us grown-ups!

Each of the animals has its own special gift or talent that every community –
be it kindergarten, school class, family or workplace – needs.

Indeed, the nine worlds taken together make the world whole.

CPSIA information can be obtained at www.ICGtesting.com
Printed in the USA
LVIW01n2115021114
411712LV00004B/8